ANTICS OF AFGHAN STREET HOUND

The Unusual Year of Darakht the Nowzad Rescue

―――

By Katherine Bennett

Blog Author, Well-Lived Life With Less

Copyright © 2018 by Katherine Bennett

All Rights Reserved.

No part of this book may be reproduced in any form or by any electronic or mechanical means, including information storage and retrieval systems, without written permission from the author, except for the use of brief quotations in a book review.

Photographs reproduced with permission from the Nowzad charity

Foreword

An Afghan animal's life is not one of comfort at the best of times; hunting for scraps of food or hiding from the hot sun during the summer and the freezing cold of an Afghan winter night. There is definitely no pampered pet status in Afghanistan. Nowzad makes a difference 'One Animal at a Time'[1].

After a three-hour flight from Kabul, an overnight stay in a Dubai rescue centre followed by an 8-hour flight to London, he is finally here. In May 2017, six months after applying to adopt a Nowzad rescue, we find ourselves driving to the Animal Reception Centre at Heathrow Airport. We are bringing home a dog we have never even met, with only photos and a couple of short videos to go on, to live with us in his forever home.

---

[1] www.justgiving.com/nowzaddogs

Why adopt a dog from Afghanistan?

Many people have asked what first inspired us to adopt a Nowzad rescue and how we came to know about the charity. For us, the answer is simple - a dog is a dog. Why should it matter where it is born? We figure that generally speaking, UK rescues have a much better chance of being adopted, a better support system in place and even strays a better quality of life,

Dave and I are both huge animal lovers, particularly dogs and have followed a number of animal charities for years. But Nowzad is different and for it has an extra place in my heart because my Dad was in the army for 22 years (there is also a strong military connection on both sides of the family). We've always had a shared but strong social conscience but, in the past, haven't always known where best to concentrate our efforts. With Nowzad, it really felt like this was something through which we could make a difference, however small in the grand scheme of things.

I discovered Pen's books in March 2014, but it was another two years before I got around to

Darakht tied to the infamous tree outside the rescue center

reading them, during which time we move house twice and get married.

That aside, I was also worried at how helpless I would feel about the dogs' plight and how upsetting the subject matter might be. And it was. Upsetting at times, that is. But the books were also incredibly uplifting and reading about how Pen has achieved what he has, and continues to do, in extremely difficult circumstances, made me think that adopting a Nowzad rescue was the very least we could do. When I eventually do pick up and start reading the first book, I am hooked. And, within a year of finishing book two, we were going through the adoption process.

Whilst we both had family pets as children I have never owned a dog of my own. The closest I've come is to dog sit a friend's Wire-haired Fox Terrier during a three-year period when I worked from home, until his death in 2014 at the ripe old age of 14; he had a good innings. Otto was the naughtiest and stubborn little dog we had ever met and at the ripe old age of 14 he had a very good innings, we loved him like our own. My husband Dave has owned a dog but not for 15+ years.

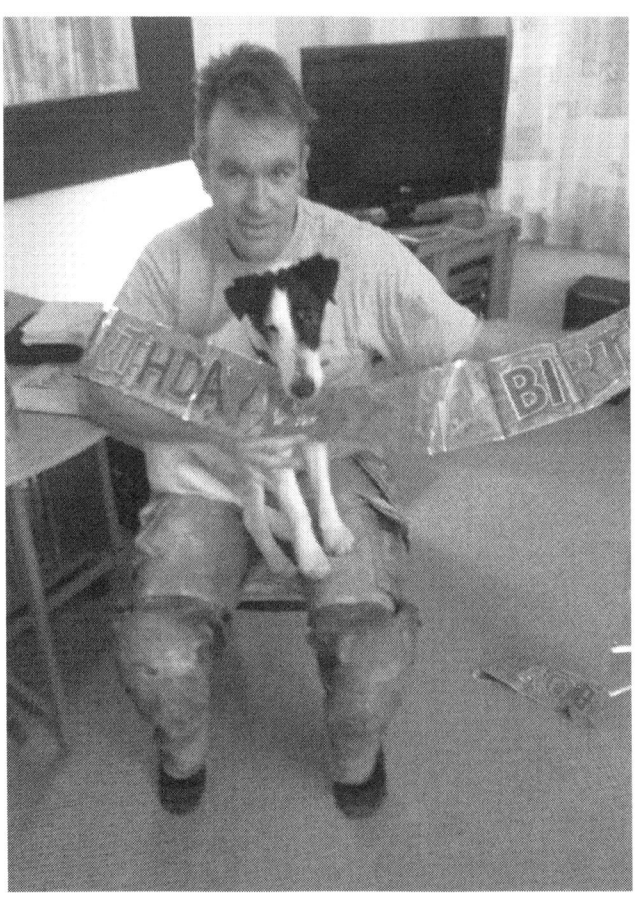

Dave and Otto on his 14th birthday

November 2016

Following countless visits to the websites of many local rescue centres, their webpages full of abandoned doggies all looking for a home, how can we possibly choose? In fact, we don't even get as far as looking at any - we just can't bring ourselves to do it.

We initially looked into a UK rescue because I assumed an overseas adoption would be a long and complicated process but once I enquire, I soon learn this isn't the case. Whilst we are told to expect a six-month wait while the charity raises the funds, the actual process is much the same as we would expect from a UK charity, i.e. matching the dog to your requirements, stating what kind of home you have, the size of your garden and how safe it is and then carrying out a home visit.

I really like how Nowzad refer to them as companion animals. In fact, they ask you to sign an agreement as part of the adoption application form stating that a dog will be rehomed as your companion and is not to be used as a guard dog. They also ask you to agree to actively take part in the fundraising process to transport your companion animal from Afghanistan to your home. I complete and send off the adoption application form. Six days later, a Nowzad volunteer in our area contacts me to arrange a home visit.

Dave is working away as always when Jen arrives at the house, so she interviews him over the phone and says she will feedback to Pen. I express concerns about leaving him alone when I am at work, but Jen says that the dogs are very happy to lie about, and we needn't worry too much about a dog sitter/dog boarding.

*****

December 2016

Ten days after Jen's home visit, we receive an email from Pen. He has sent a photo of a dog estimated to be 11 to 12 months old who loves people and other dogs. He was found abandoned outside the rescue centre and been christened Darakht, which means 'tree' in Dari, as that is what he was found tied to.

Pen asks if we would like to follow up the adoption. Darakht is fully-blood tested for entry to the UK, the charity just need to fundraise for him now. We reply within hours saying we would love to adopt him as we seem like a good match. Never in a million years do we envisage being the proud owners of a Nowzad rescue, but it could now be a reality….

Fundraising

At first, we panic because we think we have to raise the £4,000 ourselves but we quickly learn that this isn't the case. The total required for a Nowzad dog to travel to the UK is £4,000 on average – this covers the cost of adoption, retrospective care and treatment, flights, etc.

By mid-December, the charity has set up a JustGiving page, on which we learn that Darakht (pronounced 'Darak') was found by Pen and Dr. Mujtaba, Nowzad's vet. He has been well looked after who they think was a much-loved pet that somebody had to give up. Thankfully that person knew where to bring him and he has been well cared for at the Nowzad shelter ever since.

A lady called Hannah from the charity invites us to add our own paragraph to the page and we opt for the following:

We want to give Darakht a loving forever home because we fell in love with his picture on sight as did our family and friends who all can't wait to meet him! The wonderful people at Nowzad found him tied to a tree and rescued him – in fact his name means 'tree' in Dari. We have read the horrendous stories of the experiences many for the dogs in Afghanistan and really want to do our part to help as well as being able to have our own dog who we just know is going to be a loving companion for life!

Dave and I forego Christmas presents and ask our parents to donate to the JustGiving page instead. We have a second family Christmas in mid-January so my sister and brother in law and their little boy are over from Ireland. Min my sister in law asks why we decided to adopt a dog from Afghanistan. It feels like she is slightly disparaging about it but I'm sure she doesn't mean to be and I'm probably on the defensive of what seems like a crazy idea to some. And my parents-in-law seem a bit baffled but are fully supportive. Especially as Lynne, my mother-in-law previously volunteered at a local rescue centre and now in her early 70s, still carries out home visits for potential dog adopters in the UK which she has happily done for many years.

March 2017

Knowing he is nearly fully-funded only adds to our anxiety. Dave has convinced himself that Darakht isn't coming so a lot of reassurance is also needed, as we're in love with this dog even though we've yet to meet him. The fact that neither of us is a particularly patient person only exacerbates matters. In fact, we are so impatient now that we borrow Eddie, our friends Jenny and Robins' gorgeous Staffie and head down to Devon for a weekend stay at a dog-friendly pub.

Dave calls Jen to ask her about when Darakht will arrive in the UK. We get an email from Sue on the back of this, explaining that at this stage they do not know the date Darakht will be flying. They have several things to take into consideration before he can travel to the UK. Firstly, as a charity, they do not have the funds to cover the cost of his flight, so he does need to reach his goal of £4,000 before his flight can be arranged. She also says he is doing really well, so hopefully that will not be too long but as soon as they do have confirmation they will let us know. Sue thanks us for giving him this opportunity of a forever home and that he is one of the lucky ones.

Once funding is complete, they have to find somebody to travel with Darakht as all pets travelling into the UK are required to have a flight buddy that will travel with them within five days. They are hoping that somebody might be traveling to the UK in June when the funds will hopefully also have been raised.

I'm sure we're not the first anxious parents to be in regular contact but I hope that they don't find our messages too annoying. We're learning that we need to be patient in this situation, however frustrating it might be.

*****

April 2017

It is now early April and he is now over-funded at £4,152.28. An amazing 81 supporters have helped us get there and earlier than the anticipated turnaround period, thanks in no small part to our family and friends and even some of my lovely work colleagues who between us have raised £400 of the total. I post a status update on Facebook thanking everybody who has helped him get there, taking care to give a special mention to Jen Crossman and Sue Gibbs, without whose gargantuan efforts we wouldn't have reached the target.

We receive an email from Najwa, Nowzad's country manager to say that Darakht will most likely arrive on the morning of May 26. We should expect to receive an email with the exact details in early May when they book the flight and will have plenty of time to plan our time off from work.

A short time later, we hear from Najwa again. She confirms that they have a flight buddy available to travel on 23 May and would like to know if we will be able to receive Darakht then. He would depart Kabul on 23 of May and arrive sometime on 25 May. I can barely contain my excitement, but it still seems like a hundred years away.

A couple with a very cute miniature Schnauzer and another small dog sit at the table next to us and we get chatting. We inevitably tell them about Darakht and they recommend a local dog walker and boarding service called Fetch' n' Go which is where their dogs go when they are at work.

We busy ourselves with planning our summer holiday. It dawns on us even more that this is how life is going to be from now on. Wherever we go, he goes (most of the time).

*****

May 2017

How strong will he be? Will I be able to handle him? What will we feed him and in what quantities? How long will it be before he can be let off the lead? Whilst these and many other questions have permeated our thoughts in the weeks before he arrives, nothing can diminish our excitement at him finally coming.

Due to the nature of their work and time being a precious commodity, there is a three-month gap between the previous photo update of Darakht and his last, two weeks before he departs Afghanistan for his long journey to the UK, in which we saw a young dog whose paws he had yet to fully grow into at 15-months old, sat comfortably on an adult male's shoulders.

We go to the annual Christchurch food festival where there is a homemade, natural dog treats stall. I buy three packs of different treats in anticipation of his arrival. They contain all sorts of yummy ingredients like sweet potato (which we have heard dogs are partial to), salmon, etc. It occurs to me that I could easily make these myself if he likes them.

*****

The Journey Home

We've been told he should arrive on Friday 26 May. We book the time off work, but don't know even until the week he is due to travel if he will arrive on that day. The closer we get to the proposed date, the more anxious we become. I can barely concentrate at work on Wednesday and Thursday, so scared that something will go wrong.

It really could fall through at any moment. This isn't helped by the fact that we've heard a few other Nowzad adopters' stories. In Jen's case, Kabul Airport was bombed and her cat's journey to the UK had to be postponed but this isn't the most upsetting case. In some horrible instances the animal has been too unwell to travel or even died.

On the Thursday is when we know for sure he is coming. We receive an email from Dubai Kennels & Cattery/Veterinary Clinic and Animal Relocations. Tim who runs the rescue centre very kindly emails us to let us know that Darakht arrived safely last night and is doing just fine. He asks us to let them know once we have collected him tomorrow.

Another Nowzad volunteer called Ann sends me a friend request (I know she is one as these words are always in their Facebook names). She asks if we are expecting a new arrival on Friday - her adopted dog will also be on Darakht's flight.

Ann explains that there is no 'first off first out' system at the Animal Reception Centre, in fact she doesn't even think there is a system. It's a small reception, with just a vending machine, and everyone sits and waits. It could be very busy, so you just never know how long it will take.

*****

D-Day

We don't sleep much on Thursday night. We are both nervous and beyond excited and I am worried about how Darakht found the flight, consoling myself with the fact that he has come from Dubai not all the way from Kabul and was well-looked after the previous evening. He will also have been fed and provided with food and water for the journey.

We decide to travel up really early and get breakfast somewhere nearby as we don't want to risk being late, even though there is a four-hour wait. We arrive at the Animal Reception Centre at 10.00am and find a parking space. We enquire inside and are told it is another hour wait so we go for a walk. It is a hot day already and it's preferable to sitting in the car. We find some fields where we can walk to pass the time and catch our breath before our lives change for ever.

Ann messages to say they're bringing Sharifa out in 20 minutes' time, so we rush back across the vast industrial city of the airport. By the time we return to the Reception, Ann and her husband David are outside with Sharifa. I comment that Sharifa must be really shy or anxious as her head is bowed, but they tell us this is due to her injuries and I feel very ignorant. I then recall the horrendous photos Nowzad posted in 2016 and can barely believe it is the same dog.

They tell us that Billy their first Nowzad rescue, tragically died within a few months of arriving in the UK. I later learn that this was due to a neurological condition and only a very short time before getting Sharifa and I admire their kind-heartedness and compassion for adopting another Nowzad rescue so soon.

David is also a Nowzad Trustee and has recently been out to Afghanistan to see the charity's set up, which is where he first set eyes on Sharif (as she was called then – they added the 'a' at the end as she's a girl). She was born in the city of Mazar-e-Sharif and as a puppy some string was tied around her neck and got really tight as she got bigger. Living on the streets she also developed a severe case of mange so was in a really bad way. A kind person finally noticed Sharif's horrendous condition and got in touch with Nowzad where she was immediately sent to be operated on. They removed the string from her neck and treated her mange and named her Sharif after the famous Shrine of Ali in the city.

Ann and David also tell us about the adopter gatherings which happen annually. In London every November without the dogs and every summer on the south coast with the dogs (which is where we live so happy days).

I go and sit in the reception area for a while. We've checked in to let them know we are here and I ask if Darakht is okay. The lady at the desk smiles kindly and says he is doing fine. The room is full of a mix of people who have flown to Heathrow from various destinations - US service personnel (male and female), ex-pats returning from overseas and another couple around our age who look as if they are also collecting a rescue. There is a TV on in the corner of the room playing a video about the work of the Animal Reception Centre.

A short while later, somebody calls his name and I go to speak to them. He is about to be brought out. My heart is in my mouth. There are gasps as one of the ARC staff bring him through the doorway at the back of the room. Despite being underweight and in need of a good brush, his heckles up and tail between his legs and crouching as low to the floor as he possibly can, Darakht is breathtakingly beautiful and his coat is like nothing I've seen before.

He licks my face and crouches next to me, while those around me comment on how gorgeous he is. Dave comes into the room then to meet him for the first time. We take him outside where there is an artificial lawn with a small fence around it where he can safely roam and get his bearings.

Darakht's first photo shoot: outside the Animal Reception Centre

Outside, we see all the crates in which the animals have travelled in stacked high. I wonder how far each of them has come and what they have experienced. They offer us the crate Darakht travelled in to take home with us – it is enormous. Dave takes it to the car while I get a bit more acquainted with our new arrival and let him roam around the small lawn. Ann gives me a packet of natural dog treats which he seems to enjoy very much. A member of staff walking past comments that he is a gorgeous brindle, but I don't know what this is so just smile politely and say thank you.

Scrawny but safe: grass outside the Animal Reception Centre

The crate is too big for the car, but we figure Darakht may not welcome going back inside it anyway, so he takes the water bowl instead and takes the crate back to the stack. Besides, we have an estate so there's plenty of room for the dog in the boot. Dave also fitted the dog guard and put his new bed in there before we left so he'll be perfectly safe and comfortable.

Getting him into the car is a different story as he point blank refuses to get into the boot, choosing to stay rooted to the spot on the hot tarmac. After ten minutes of failed attempts, Ann suggests picking him up. Thankfully he lets Dave do this without much of a protest and soon Darakht is settled in the boot in his new bed. Ann and David are ready to take their own new arrival home, so we wish them luck and wave them goodbye.

It is only a couple of hours drive back to Bournemouth, so he doesn't need to be in the car for too long. I spend half of the journey craning my neck into the back of the car to check he's okay.

*****

From Kabul to Claremont Avenue

Darakht sniffs the south coast air with unbridled suspicion. His new environment is comprised of strange smells and tastes, flora and fauna and unfamiliar noises. It is immediately apparent that he is an opportunist when it comes to any food that isn't meant for him, with that look in his eyes of animals forced to scavenge and use their wits to survive. Whilst he isn't actually feral, he certainly comes close in many ways. The stairs in our house are a different matter. He has clearly never encountered them before.

When he isn't roaming our back garden, he is lying in any dirt he can find which is mainly our flower borders. Accustomed to 40° temperatures, we assume this is the normal way for a dog to cool itself down in the middle east. We know from Jen that the temperature in Afghanistan can be either unbearably hot or unbearably cold with extremes of 40° either way. It can rain so hard out there which some dogs find painful and Jen has told us that her dog Chica doesn't like going for a walk in the rain as she expects this to still be the case.

Darakht hiding in the dirt in our back garden

There is no way of ascertaining Darakht's quality of life prior to Nowzad untying him from that tree. Now, lying in our garden, Darakht seems fairly relaxed – hard to reconcile with.... We're just grateful that he was kept safe from the daily dangers he would be subjected to on the streets. When I imagine what Sharifa went through it doesn't bear thinking about – who knows what could have become of him if they hadn't got that call.

*****

Darakht staking out his new back garden for the first time

We take him to Moors Valley Country Park. We've never been there but lots of people have recommended it as a big space ideal for walking a dog and it's only a short drive away. A squirrel sets him off on a frenzy of barking and seemingly pointless running around. He's only been with us for a week but Darakht has quickly worked out what our car looks like and that a sit-down protest shortly before we reach it is very effective. After several failed attempts to get him to stand up, Dave has no option but to carry him to the car.

I text my friend Kathleen to arrange a doggy date for Darakht and Jack, her gorgeous little black rescue. Prior to him, she was the proud owner of lovely Otto for 14 years. We were hoping to use the same dog walker/sitter as Kathleen, but it isn't going to be possible. She does offer to have him on her days off but as she lives in the opposite direction to work I can't see this working. So, it's over to Plan B.

*****

Doggy Day Care

I do some online research for local day care services and come across NarpsUK (National Association of Pet Sitters & Dog Walkers) and The Good Dog Guide. I shortlist four, including Julie from Fetch 'n Go who was recommended by the couple in the pub. I contact them and say we have just adopted a rescue dog from the Nowzad charity in Afghanistan whom we collected from Heathrow the previous Friday. We are looking for local day care for him during the week while we're at work (potentially 3-4 days per week). We are ideally looking for help w/c 12 June, however a couple of weeks after that would be okay as we have family and friends who can help out in the short-term. I say I appreciate it is potentially short notice, but we only had final confirmation of his flight date a few days before, due to the nature of the charity's work and where they are based.

One of them responds to say she would love to help with our new dog and is a keen Nowzad supporter. However, she thinks it would only confuse him to arrive at our house and then keep coming to her for the odd day. She has tried this before and the poor dog couldn't cope so we had to call it a day. If we are still looking for somewhere in a months' time, then by all means come back to her and we can try it out.

I find this a bit condescending and I feel like a neglectful parent, even though I was clear in my email what we are looking for. I reply that it wouldn't just be the odd day and my parents are having him most likely every Friday, so we are looking for three to four other fixed days per week. I add that I understand about confusion, but he really is the most chilled out dog and attach some photos. I ask if there's any way she could meet him anyway, so she can see what he's like, even if we don't come back to her for a month. She replies saying that I am very welcome to come and meet her and I arrange this for the end of the week.

One provider doesn't have a website or email address, just a Facebook Page so I contact her via that. This seems a bit unprofessional, but she is listed on The Good Doggy Guide website and licensed by Bournemouth Council, so I dismiss this as pernickety on my part. She responds quickly saying she has availability and I can come round to the house to meet her and see the set up. She only lives up the road so this is sounding great. I arrange to meet her on Thursday 1 June.

*****

June 2017

Jude's house is not at all what I was expecting. She lives in a small terrace with a narrow back garden separated into different sections. She tells me that the dog will only be allowed in the small front yard in the first part of the garden. At the back of my mind, I am questioning how easy both her immediate availability and lack of inquisitive about his situation is. This is in stark contrast to the lady who questioned Darakht's confusion, who at least was honest and not just interested in taking my money regardless of what was in the best interests of our rescue dog. But I'm so relieved to have found someone that I go ahead anyway as I need to sort this out before peternity leave is up.

Dave and I take Darakht for a walk along Boscombe Overcliff and then meet some of the girls from work at Urban Reef on the seafront. He is clearly overwhelmed by all the people there and Dave is keen to only stay for one drink, so they leave shortly afterwards. He has really missed the dog while he's been working away so I know he wants to have him all to himself for a few hours and rightly so.

It's Sunday and Philip arrives with our good friends Maz and Rosie. He is a cousin of Rosie's whose boss has sent him to do an English language course in Bournemouth, so he will be staying with us for the duration. As much as we love seeing their dogs Milou and Daisy, we are relieved that they don't have their dogs with them as they are exceptionally small. We leave them to it and take Darakht to Mum and Dad's for dinner where he also gets to meet Robert and his girlfriend Angela who have both followed his, and our, journey to get him here with great interest.

I don't sleep very well during my week's peternity leave as I am constantly checking he is breathing. As I always do with those that I love the most in the world, I worry that something bad will happen to them. Now I understand how parents must feel.

As Jen predicted, Darakht spends a lot of time sleeping. He also seems to have boundless energy one minute and is crashed out the next, although I expect he'll burn some of it off once we take him off the lead in a couple of weeks' time. He is also very fond of spinning around in circles or bowing when he wants to play which I learn is a way of showing happiness. I have never seen a dog do this before which all adds to his exoticness.

Already his nails are long and need clipping, so I take him to The Groom Room which is part of Pets at Home. He isn't very happy about it but is very well-behaved and doesn't protest when they clip his claws. I later learn that I can get them clipped for free at the vets which proves a much nicer experience.

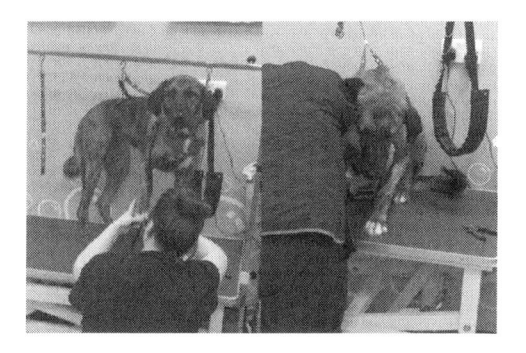

During his peternity leave the following week, Dave takes Darakht to meet the Bennett grandparents. When we next see Dick and Lynne, they comment that he seemed to have already bonded well with Dave during that visit as he was looking for him every time he left the room and seemed very settled, which is lovely to hear. We wanted to make sure that Darakht got to meet both sets of grandparents within his first two weeks and he is immediately at ease and at home with them, as we would have expected.

Somebody tells us about a dog training park at Slades Farm where Darakht can be let off the lead safely. It provides safe exercise and play equipment in a special fenced off area that includes an obstacle course and seating. During the week, Dave texts me at work with a photo of Darakht stood very regally in the middle of the training park without his lead on. It is a proud moment.

Getting him in and out of the car is still proving an issue but Dave does some online research, settling on a Cesar dog training video which offers some good tips. Darakht is soon hopping in and out of the boot and we breathe a collective sigh of relief particularly as we have a long drive to North Wales next month. We put it down to now associating it with nice things like going for a walk.

I hear back from Julie at Fetch 'n' Go on 11 June but it's too late as Monday 12 June is Darakht's first day at Jude's. The handover goes as smoothly as it can and Jude is there to greet him at the front door.

I am experiencing horrendous mothers' guilt for leaving him with a stranger in an unfamiliar environment and worry that he thinks he has been abandoned again. But this seems like the kindest option, better at least than leaving him home alone.

I am also very conscious that life in the Nowzad shelter was spent with a couple of kennel mates and he isn't accustomed to being on his own. I do joke several times about him needing company but so far Dave is not taking the bait. Give it time.

As the week goes on, the mornings consist of getting to Jude's, coaxing him out of the car and dragging him up the path. A series of lying down protests ensue which I cannot do anything about as he is too strong, but I put this down to separation anxiety and persevere.

The next time I collect him, Jude tells me that her son and his family live in the house opposite ours. This is the man who insists on revving the engine of a clapped-out VW Beetle late at night on week nights (with three young children of his own in the house) while he 'repairs' it. We have been moaning to each other about this since we moved here in August 2016. Two dogs can also be heard barking each time somebody enters or leaves their house but (to this day) I have never seen them taken for a walk. Oh, the irony – a lack of emotional intelligence is an emerging theme here.

When I collect him on Wednesday, Jude tells me she told him off for eating a packet of cheddars left on the kitchen side. I apologise of course, but back home I decide that the dog is not to blame. Notwithstanding the fact that he has been in the country all of three weeks and is also a rescued street dog with a complicated relationship with food. Surely a dog sitter who is accustomed to other people's dogs in her home should be mindful of leaving food out, but I let it lie.

Dave also wants to meet her, so we arrange to go to the house. He is not particularly happy about the fact that Darakht is only allowed in a small part of the garden which I obviously agree with. Back at home we agree that it isn't working and we need to move him to a nearer sitter before he gets too used to the other place. I email Julie and say that we are thinking of moving Darakht at the end of the summer and can we arrange to meet. Dave happens to be home on Monday evening, so this would be ideal.

*****

Monday 19 June. Jude doesn't seem to be around, in fact I don't see her all week. Her husband who isn't particularly friendly at the best of times, doesn't even explain why which makes me feel even more uneasy. And, if she isn't around, how is he being looked after bearing in mind that the husband walks with the aid of a stick and uses a motability scooter.

In the evening we walk to Julie's to get Darakht accustomed to the route. When we arrive, he walks straight up to front door and into the house. We cannot believe the difference and we think we've definitely made the right decision.

At the weekend we go and see the Stone Roses at Wembley, which is a welcome distraction from everything. Darakht has his first sleepover at my Mum and Dad's where he already feels very at home so we know we can properly relax.

Relaxing with Grandad Roy in their back garden

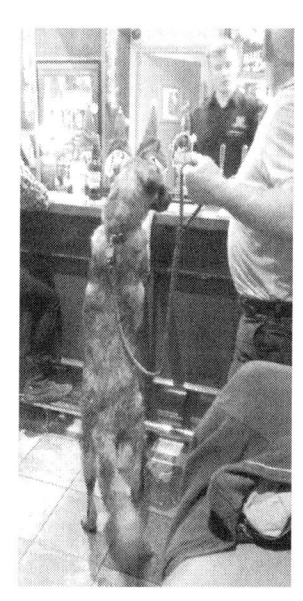

A regular trip to Mum & Dad's local

Tuesday 20 June. Julie emails to say how happy she is that we have chosen to use Fetch 'n' Go. She and her daughter both think Darakht is a beautiful boy and she knows her husband and son will fall in love with him too. As for Maddie (who is the same build as Darakht), she thinks they will become best buddies, while Bess will just stay in the background and keep watch. She also says she was a bit concerned that Darakht has not wanted to go into the house of the lady he is with at the moment, but this could just be nerves or separation anxiety, after all he has been through more than his fair share in his short life.

Darakht resting after a long walk with Maddie and Katie

She thinks it will be okay for Darakht as most dogs have a very good memory for places, but we are more than welcome to pop round with him a few times before then, so he can familiarise himself with them and the dogs a bit more. She was also amazed at how well he and Maddie got on and how relaxed he seemed, so we are obviously doing a good job with him. We arrange another meeting for the end of June so that her husband Steve can also meet us and Darakht, as he also helps out with the business. The meeting goes well and everybody is happy to go ahead from mid-July. As we'll be on holiday until late July this dovetails really nicely.

Darakht with Dave & Philip at our local

Now that we have made the decision to move, I am fretting about what to say to Jude. Dave is away again now so I talk it through with Philip. This straight-talking Venezuelan thinks I should just be upfront with her. The truth be told, I am scared of telling her I am leaving and then having to go back there the next day, especially if I am going to be greeted at the door by her grumpy husband more often than not.

*****

My great friend Lyndsey's Mum is over from Thailand and it'll be great to see her as it's been a few years. Heidi and her husband Alan run a luxury villa on the island of Koh Tao where they have lived for a couple of decades and where we travelled to when Lynds and Terry got married back in 2010.

Heidi has followed Darakht's progress on Facebook and I know she desperately wants to meet him. He also reminds her of their old dog Remi who also had a brindle coat. Heidi and Alan are strong advocates for sustainability and environmental issues. Heidi is also heavily involved n the programme to rid Koh Tao of rabies and regularly travels the island with her veterinary friend inoculating the stray dogs against the disease as the island currently enjoys rabies-free status.

Heidi and Darakht getting acquainted

Heidi and Lynds come over to the house and by the end of the visit Heidi would like to take him home with her. As I'm stood in the doorway waving them off, Darakht escapes and runs off down the street. My heart is in my mouth. The closer to the end of the road he gets the more scared I am as it goes straight onto a really busy road and he has zero road sense.

It's thanks to Lynds quick-thinking that he comes back at all. Remembering how much he loves his squeaky toy she stands outside the house squeezing it as if her life depends on it, until he comes running back up the street to a stern telling off. But this is still remarkable considering he had clearly never encountered a squeaky toy until a couple of days ago

*****

I have a plan. I message Jude to say that Mum and Dad are going to look after the dog on weekdays and that it was never my intention to mess her about, but I wasn't expecting them to offer. I want to give her as much notice as possible so his last day will be Thursday 13 July if that's okay with her. She replies to say this is fine and a wait is lifted off my shoulders.

We ask in our local pet shop if they can recommend a nearby dog training class and they tell us about one in a church hall by the shopping centre down the road from us. I enroll him onto the beginners' class at Kadarow Dog Training as soon as we get home. Katie the owner emails me back to say that she knows the Nowzad charity very well and is thrilled to have one of their lovely dogs attend her Beginner Course. She wishes us all the best with Darakht's continued settling in period and looks forward to meeting us on 27 June.

Out walking Darakht a few days later, I meet a lady with a lively Spaniel puppy who is also going to the class as the trainer has been recommended to her by other dog walkers so I'm feeling very positive about it. It's also nice as we don't know many people in the area so having a dog will be one of the many things that this helps with.

It's his first class tonight. I see Claire who I met while walking the dog in Muscliffe Park. Her little spaniel is a live wire but very sweet. Darakht wows everybody with his exceptional placidness, sitting like a sphinx and observing all the other dogs running around madly. Katie is impressed at how settled and comfortable he is and of course he takes a liking to her straight away, particularly when he knows she is the purveyor of the tastiest treats in the room.

Darakht's certificate from his first Dog Training Course

July 2017

Monday 3 July. Normally Darakht will get out of the car and then slowly up the path with treats. This morning he wouldn't get out of the car without a lot of persuasion and refused to come to the door, so even the treats aren't working now. It shouldn't be this difficult and I've had enough. I walk back down the path, put him back in the car and drive home, not caring that I will now be late for work.

I message Jude to say I think it's best if I keep Darakht at home as it is stressing both of us out too much; in any case, we are paid up to 14 July. She replies that she hopes he can 'get over his issues and de-stress' and wishes us good luck. Her response shows that even if I had been honest with her, she wouldn't have taken any responsibility. I am emotionally drained and just relieved I don't have to go back, so leave things there.

When I do eventually get to work, I call Dave to let him know what's happened. We agree that we can manage until we go on holiday with a bit of help from Mum and Dad and me popping home to check on him. I'm lucky that the main campus of Bournemouth University (BU) where I work is a ten-minute drive away, so I can easily get home at lunchtimes.

I now start worrying that the son will see Julie coming and going and report back to Jude. This is silly I know, as how is he to know that Julie isn't my Mum? I know I'm being paranoid, but my nerves are shot to pieces and I'm not thinking rationally. Philip just laughs at me.

I create a WhatsApp group so that Dave can see the regular updates, photos and videos Julie has regularly been sending. He really misses the dog when he's working away and doesn't want to miss out on his progress.

Over the next few weeks however, it becomes apparent that we are in need of intervention and Julie is struggling and the last thing we want is to lose her help. Her husband recommends an ex-police colleague called Colin who used to train police dogs. As the UK police force use Belgian Shepherds these days this could work really well. We get in touch and arrange in late July when we are back from our holiday.

Today we are travelling from Bournemouth to Barmouth for a well-earned break. While we're enjoying our holiday, I receive a message from Jude via Facebook asking if I can write a review on her Facebook page. At first I'm quite angry, but then we see the funny side and have a good laugh about it. I don't oblige.

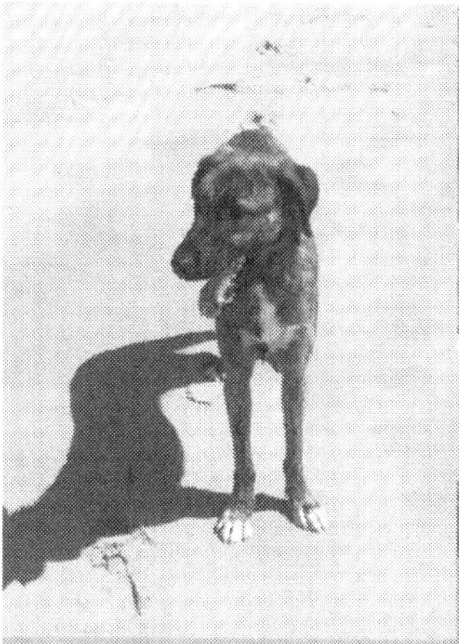
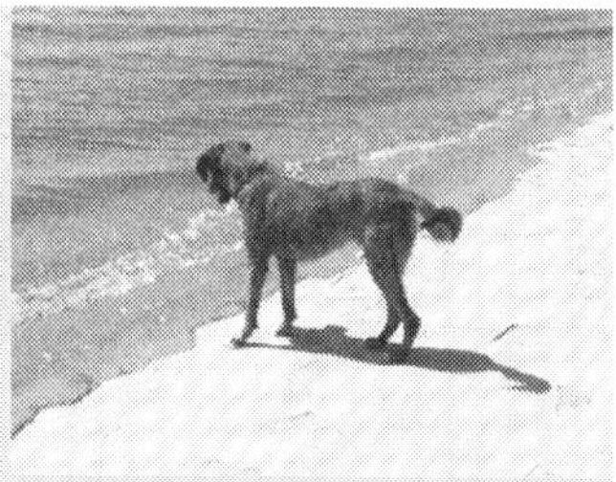
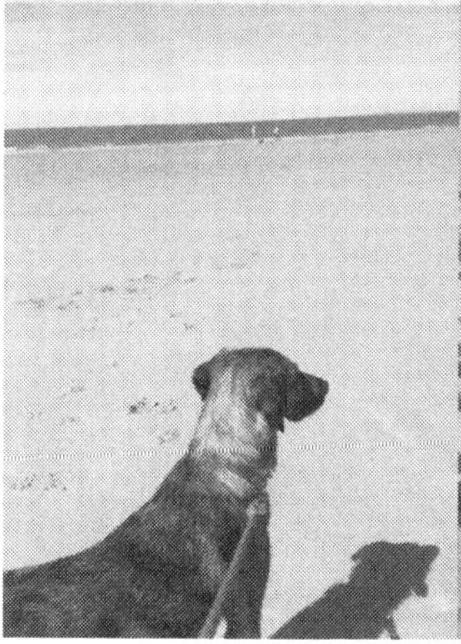
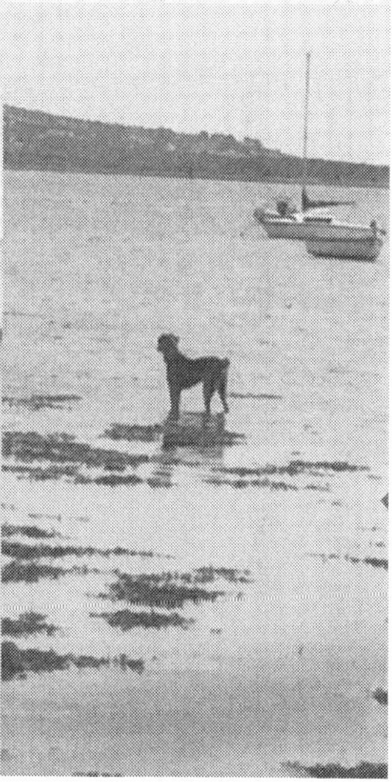

Darakht and the Police Dog Trainer

On Colin's first visit to the house he tells us in no uncertain terms how things are from a legal standpoint. This puts the fear of God into us, but this isn't necessarily a bad thing.

Colin is a strong advocate for natural dog food which is music to my ears as I have been considering this for Darakht. What is not music to my ears however, is him not being sympathetic to us adopting a rescue dog from abroad which he vocalises his opinion on a few times. He is also critical of the dog trainers' methods, but we are quickly learning that like many things, you will encounter several contradictory theories on what's best for your dog and just have to go with what feels right for you.

Darakht is understandably very well-socialised with other dogs which makes things easier to manage, but the children issue is exacerbated by the fact that they we just don't spend much time with them ourselves – they only come to the house once in a blue moon. We can only surmise that he was mistreated by children back home. I know of several instances of this happening, the most extreme stories being Chica who was rescued from a group of children who were trying to sever one of her back legs – she still bears the scar.

Colin's theory is that he is not able to distinguish between children and small animals and the fact that they are unpredictable noisy, wave their arms about, etc. however, one thing which Colin and Katie both suggest is spending time where there are lots of children so that Darakht can observe them. This is definitely going to be a long game.

Darakht starts his intermediate dog training course tonight. We arrive with him wearing the lead Colin sold to us, but Katie is not impressed and says she doesn't agree with those types of leads. I feel like a neglectful parent again and the lead is banished to the back of a cupboard. We are actually relieved as we have felt cruel using it on him and it has made his behavior worse not better. As soon as we put him back on his other lead, his behavior is markedly improved. He is still naughty, but it is a more manageable kind and there is no biting.

We feel that Colin is treating him like a police recruit and it's making us uncomfortable. Whilst our motivation for seeking the help of a dog behaviorist in the first place was because of Darakht's relationship with children. However, first and foremost he is a pet and a companion animal. We cancel the August appointment and agree to ask for Katie's previously offered help instead (she also does one-on-one training).

The application form we completed stated that Nowzad dogs are not aware of traffic or able to easily adapt to busy main roads with carful and constant supervision. Ain't that the truth. Darakht will happily walk out in front of an approaching car. It's as if he just doesn't see them but I guess I would be the same if I had spent the majority of my life in a rescue centre.

Darakht has his first UK vet check. The vet is very interested in his back story and says he will do some research to check that there aren't any other nasties he needs to be inoculated against.

A 17-year old Ukrainian called Vlad arrives today and we have further bookings for Italian and

German students of the same age, in addition to Philip. Having other people in the house, particularly international students, is a shot in the dark but we need to pay for the £200 a month dog boarding/walking plus other expenses of dog ownership somehow. Darakht has started spending Fridays at Mum and Dad's which helps cost wise. More importantly, it's comforting to know he's with family at least for one day I am at work.

Over the next few months, various Nowzad volunteers or fellow adopters get in touch, either by dropping us an email or sending a friend request. It really makes me feel like part of the family!

*****

August 2017

During the course of their two walks a day, Julie is having real problems when getting him back to our house, in that he is either refusing to get out of the car or go into the house (even with treats). He is snapping when she tries to move him and she is having to phone her husband to come and help her. He is also sitting down on walks and refusing to budge – the average sit-down protest is ten minutes; the record is thirty!

Julie WhatsApps again about him sitting down protests on walks and this time sends a video. I forward this and her message to Colin who says that she is praising him for not doing what she wants him to do, for doing what he is doing, which is refusing to move. He says his collar is also too loose so therefore not effective in instilling a little control over him. The mouthing he is doing at the moment is also a protest and using it to his advantage. He agrees it sounds like an abandonment/separation anxiety issue as he has learnt that he is being left alone for a period of time. Colin suggests muzzle training him initially so that he cannot learn to use his teeth to get what he wants (to be left in the car) and would not risk Julie getting bitten for the sake of it. With regards to sitting down and refusing to move, he would not accept this from Darakht. He needs to be encouraged to walk forward with the use of a short lead, by giving him a stern pull forward and praising as soon as he moves.

One of the rear brake lights on the car has blown so we swing by Halfords to get a new one. One of the staff comes outside to fit it for us but as soon as he puts his hand in the boot to get to it, Darakht nips his hand. It is mortifying but all we can do is apologise and pray that the doesn't want to take it further. He doesn't so I get Darakht out of the boot and at a safe distance so that he can get on with the job. Incidents like this need to be carefully monitored and pre-empted where possible.

Julie has been in touch again. Most days we are getting a bad report on his behavior. We go to her house to discuss what to do. We state that we in no way are trying to persuade her to carry on looking after him if she's not comfortable, but she is insistent that she perseveres. Steve suggests some software which will enable us to watch what he's up to when we're out. The most difficult part for us is that this behavior just hasn't been our experience, or that of my parents when they look after him. We tell her to not be afraid of being firmer with him.

By the middle of the month we have decided we need to take a break from students as we feel it's unsettling Darakht. In fact, this hiatus lasts until February 2018 in the end.

*****

You are what you eat

Darakht has a funny relationship with food. When it's offered to him he takes it very gently from your hand or is very good at sitting and waiting until you say it's okay for him to eat it. When it comes to any food that isn't meant for him, he is snappy and predatory around anything in the bin, on the kitchen side or the dining room table. We buy bins with locks on them which are still necessary a year on.

Pen serving dinner at the Nowzad shelter

Commercial dog food is hard to come by in Afghanistan. From the age of six months when Darakht was rescued, his diet has been a "daily soup of rice, naan bread, meat, carrots and potatoes"[2]. Having both been brought up on meals cooked from scratch and eating leftovers, extending this mentality to our pet was a natural step.

Whilst we feel out of touch with what is beyond the supermarket/big chain pet stores, we know what we don't want to feed him, which seems like a good starting point. We refuse point blank to feed him tinned dog meat but have little knowledge of what else is available. So, we buy kibble on the advice of our local pet shop for the first couple of months.

Pretty quickly however, the natural and raw diets I start reading about and convince Dave will be best for him, we discover are far easier to acquire than we thought and by August Darakht is off the kibble, the former foodstuff not wasted but to be used as training treats. As I have read about many times

---

[2] www.nowzad.com/our-work/our-shelter

since, diet does affect dog behaviour in the same way that it does children and the detrimental effects of the kibble further strengthened our resolve.

Now, I won't pretend that our decision isn't met with an element of trepidation. Whilst we know that a Nowzad dog's diet is natural and non-processed, it will be a while before we can recognise if any changes in him are due simply to eating differently in the UK or to the quality (or not) of his food.

We needn't have worried. The changes are highly visible and almost immediate. On the kibble diet, he constantly drinks water and is hyperactive. And, when he isn't pooing four or five times a day, he is bloated and immediately starts farting for England. On the raw/natural diet, he drinks little and often, is not hyperactive straight after a meal, poos a couple of times a day max. and doesn't have diarrhea. His teeth are also in great condition, i.e. white and free of plaque.

Unless he's eaten something questionable out on a walk, horse manure being a snack of choice, he doesn't have bad breath either. In fact, a year after having him and at no time having been subjected to a bath, one of the customers in our local pub comments that he likes our dog because he never smells. We mainly feed him minced chicken (DEFRA approved), the ultimate dog superfood containing meat, cartilage, offal and bone (raw chicken bones are safe as they don't splinter). We buy this from our local raw dog food supplier at only £1.60 per 1kg pack which is the equivalent of three meals.

Most weekends we either roast or poach a whole chicken. Pies, stir fries and sandwich fillings are just some of the meals one large £5.00 bird can provide us with. The rich stock we are left with from putting the carcass back in the slow cooker not only works as a great base for risottos, but Darakht goes mad for the 'slimy' leftovers of skin and other unidentifiable bits of chicken (minus the cooked bones, of course). We regularly supplement his meals with brown rice or pearl barley, sweet potatoes, peas, apples, carrots and iron-rich greens such as kale, cabbage and sprout tops all of which he really enjoys. We want to vary his diet as much as possible but with a high degree of consistency in terms of being raw or natural.

As a result, he produces white poo which crumbles something I've not seen much of since I was a child which I think is because the average western dog's diet today seems to be predominantly processed, at least if the vets, supermarkets and TV adverts are anything to go by. As we have been making a concerted effort to eliminate even more processed foods from our own diet, we want to start as we mean to go on with the dog.

This approach is also linked to our 'less' philosophy which my blog Well-Lived Life With Less is all about. In Darakht's case, it is about less waste, less processed food less money unnecessarily spent on dog food which isn't necessarily good for him. In my view, feeding him the most natural food we can is one of the kindest things we can do.

*****

October 2017

We are walking on the beach trying to be vigilant with treats in hand and lead poised to put back on him. The problem however is we don't have a hope in hell of catching him once he starts running. It all happens in slow motion as he spots a child running up the beach back to his parents on the promenade. Darakht shoots after the boy and launches himself at the child, nipping the top of his head. The child looks understandably shocked but unhurt and luckily for us his parents are not facing in the same direction.

Unfortunately, he is like a greyhound after a hare and as soon as he has a target in his sights, there is no stopping or catching him. The more we call him, the more he ignores us. I am now not comfortable walking him on the beach my own and

*****

November 2017

Since April I have been covering the maternity leave of a colleague. The post is only until December however I have known for a few months that Caroline would like to come back to work part-time. I really enjoy my job and there really isn't any other job I want to do at the university at the present time and looking outside of BU is definitely not a prospect I relish.

I discuss the job-share opportunity with Dave and the fact that this would mean working part-time. I am extremely pleasantly surprised by his reaction. He is happy for me to do it and says that I can do anything I set my mind too. I love my husband more than ever right now.

We're also ready to rent the downstairs en-suite again as Darakht is now incredibly settled which is best demonstrated when he moans and groans with satisfaction when he's lying on one of his various day beds. He's also a joy when he's well-behaved, much like a human toddler. Most weeks I am rattling around in our four-bedroom house on my own, so we may as well utilise a great source of passive income.

I create accounts on Airbnb, Homestay and Spare Room and also arrange for us to be added to the homestay lists of both Bournemouth University and its neighbour, Arts University Bournemouth. Our current thinking is that a long-term stay would be best as we don't yet know how Darakht is going to be.

Bonfire Night passes without event. We have gone to the lengths of me staying home and missing a good friend's 40th birthday but he is completely unfazed by loud noises, bangs, etc. which speaks volumes. Still, we would never have given ourselves if we had both gone out and he had been distressed.

*****

It's all about the 11th

On the 11th day of the 11th month, we will remember them….

We have bought tickets for our first Nowzad event which is really exciting. It also happens to be the charity's 11th anniversary. Ann invites us to join them at the SWA Remembrance Sunday service for Animals in War which they are all attending tomorrow at the Animal Memorial on Park Lane. Dave wants to get back to Bournemouth to spend a bit of time with the dog and urges me to go anyway, but I'm too shy to go along on my own. Hopefully we can go next year instead.

nowzad
Winning the War for Animals

IT'S ALL ABOUT THE 11TH

11 Years of Nowzad

11th November 2017
The Audley
Bitter Sling Basement Bar
41-43 Mount Street
London
W1K 2RX

6.30pm - 12.00pm (Pen's talk will start at 7.45pm prompt)

During the day we go to Borough Market and for a drink in the Shard restaurant on the 31st floor, so it has been a great day rounded off with a very special evening I am proud to attend.

The event happens to be in The Audley in Mayfair which happens to be a few doors down from Majestic Wine, one of the four London stores I worked in during my time as a Graduate Management trainee with the company.

We descend the steps into the basement bar and I immediately regret not arriving earlier. The place is really busy and quite dark and I only recognise Pen, Hannah and David who is deep in conversation with somebody. I say hello as I go past anyway but I don't think he remembers me at first.

I busy myself with pretending to choose which wine to drink when it will only ever be Pinot Grigio rose. I swear blind that René's girlfriend in 'Allo 'Allo, the actress Vicky Michelle is stood next to me at the bar. Dave doesn't believe me but I later find out that it is indeed her. Having also spotted Peter Egan, a patron of Nowzad who appeared in

Chariots of Fire, the evening is proving to be very surreal on many levels.

Pen gives a talk and hear the stories I have read about in his books in person. He has dedicated his life to Nowzad and just exudes compassion and care for animals. It's also great to hear how things have progresses since Pen wrote the books and about the projects they are currently working on. A lady who runs the charity Animals Asia also gives an inspiring talk.

Dave is urging me to talk to Pen but I need some more Dutch courage. He's also permanently surrounded by people who want to talk to him. Dave spots a window and goes and speaks to Pen himself. I shyly approach but unsurprisingly Pen is very warm and inviting, hugging and thanking me for adopting one of their rescues.

A snatched but blurry photo opp during a rare moment when Pen isn't surrounded by people

Pen calls Hannah over to tell her that we're the couple who adopted Darakht, whom they both fondly remember. He pronounces it 'Darash' and I worry we have been mispronouncing his name all this time, but it's too late now. Besides, more often than not we use one of his pet names - Darakht, aka Big Lad, Big Guy, Puppalicious, Pupster, Puppers, Tiger and Monkey Face (my brother's nickname for him).

I show them the picture of him in front of Terry and Lynds' fireplace as I think this photo personifies his new life and his happiness.

We spend a bit more time chatting and Hannah tells me that there are people who actually return the dogs to them which I am appalled and heartbroken by. She also asks if I would be interested in acting as a contact for other people looking to adopt a Nowzad rescue to which I respond that I would love to help, of course.

We enter the raffle and win a three-month supply of Beautiful Joe's Ethical Dog Treats. They are an artisan dog food producer whose 'perfectly behaved' treats are hand-made from British free-range ox liver and slowly dried to lock in the flavour. They have very little scent and actually look like pieces of dark chocolate. New subscribers also receive a snazzy free tin with their first order.

For every packet sold, Beautiful Joe's also donate a packet to a canine rescue centre. Nominated by their customers. Most rescue centres can't afford to buy natural dog treats for the dogs they look after, let alone air-dried, pure liver treats.

Rescue centres mainly use them to train their rescue dogs so that it's easier for them to find new, forever homes. If that wasn't enough, Beautiful Joe's also donate 1% of sales to Compassion in World Farming. We like them already and we haven't received the treats yet. On paper though, they sound delicious from Darakht's viewpoint.

*****

December 2017

After successfully reapplying for my own job, I let Julie know that I'm going to be part-time from January. I feel bad as between us we have invested a lot of time getting Darakht to where he is now. Nevertheless, we can't afford to keep paying her now that I am part-time and want to look after my own dog on the days I am working from home. On the days I'm at the university I can take him out before work and pop home at lunchtimes to check on him. I can't quite reconcile this with my carbon footprint, but at least I can offset a sedentary vocation against regular walks in the fresh air and the free exercise this offers.

In mid-December we receive a lovely email from Pen saying how fab it was to meet us both in London and thanking us for coming along to the event. He asks how Darakht is doing and says that we are both amazing for giving him the chance and opportunity to be part of a family.

It is Jonnie and Min's turn to host the Bennett Christmas. We started looking into ferry crossings and dog-friendly hotels in Wales where we can stop overnight to break the journey up for Darakht. We also bought a dog crate as we were anxious about how he would be around the children. Percy met Darakht at Dick's 70th birthday weekend back in December and whilst his comment that he didn't like the way the dog was looking at his sandwich was adorable, it highlighted the impracticality of Christmas at their house this year.

More importantly, our niece Daisy was only born in mid-October and it would not be fair on Min who would of course not be able to relax properly while he was there. Nor would we, so we made the decision not to go to Ireland this year. My mother-in-law comments that she hopes this isn't the end of Bennett Christmases, but I reassure her that it won't be. We will go another time when Percy and Daisy are both a bit older. And, as Dave says, it is Darakht's first Christmas and there is no way we won't spend it with him. I am reminded of my Emily's comment that they come as a three when we said that children weren't invited about our wedding – I completely get it now, Emily!

We go to Mum and Dad's Christmas for instead, where all we need to worry about is what food Darakht can reach or get his paws on. I have gone completely overboard and bought him several (practical) presents and a stocking to hang with ours in front of the fireplace, stuffed full of impractical presents.

*****

January to February 2018

After a few false starts with renting our ensuite bedroom, an English guy gets in touch who is after a three to six month stay while he relocates to Bournemouth and buys a property. Oli seems very nice and he and his girlfriend are both very taken with Darakht which is what matters more to us.

We also hear from the agency Marco the Italian student came through, that he would like to come back in August which is great news. It will be interesting to see what changes he notices in Darakht in the twelve months since he last saw him, when the dog was a very new addition to the family.

Darakht is loving the fact that I am at home more often and taking him on all his weekday walks. One of his favourite habits is to wait until Dave's van has driven away and jump on the bed which never fails to make me chuckle.

Part-time working life is going really well so far. Between looking after Dave's admin and learning how to monetise my blog Well-Lived Life With Less, we really aren't doing too badly at all. This book actually started life as a blog but I decided in the end that I needed to tell his story and that of the Nowzad charity properly.

*****

March 2018

On and off since October Darakht has had various bouts of sore and weepy eyes and we have been back and forth to the vet five or six times so far. Dave takes him for another check-up and when they get back, he tells me that the vet has found early signs of cataracts. This is very upsetting to hear but they've detected it in good time and he just needs to be monitored. The trials and tribulations of unusual flora and fauna, I guess.

What did we find to talk about over the phone before the hound came into our lives? Our phone conversations these days seem to be dominated by how the dog is, what he's been doing and so on. Everywhere we go, Darakht still attracts a lot of attention. What breed is he? Is he a girl or a boy? So, you went over there and brought him back with you? Were you in the Forces?

Belgian Shepherd, Afghan Wolfhound, Afghan Herding Dog, Lurcher, Saluki, Anatolian Shepherd. These are just a few of the dog breeds the people we meet when we're out and about have suggested he is. I would still love to know his genetic make-up for all sorts of reasons - health, character traits and temperament being the main ones. The search is still very much on for a reputable provider of DNA testing. Watch this space for our progress on this!

April 2018

On a positive note, this month we welcome our first international students since Marco went home to Italy last September. Alex and Nuria are both Spanish but are separate bookings and not known to each other.

Any concerns about the dog dissolve as soon as they arrive. He hangs out in their rooms, plays with them, licks their faces and it's a delight. Nuria is infatuated with Darakht and throughout the month she is with us, he has been the star of many photos, WhatsApp messages to me while I am at work and Facetime calls to her Mum. She even offers to take Darakht for a walk on more than one occasion.

Dave and I go on a rare trip to the cinema to watch Isle of Dogs, the irony of which is not lost on us. We book the early evening screening as now we're in our early 40s we like to be near home at a decent time and also, we don't like being back late for the dog. We go for a couple of drinks after the film but the parental guilt sets in and we worry that he is home alone in the dark as it was still light when we left the house. When we get home, the dog is nowhere to be seen initially and the house seems to be in darkness. He then emerges from Nuria's room where she tells us he has been lying on her bed. I'm going to have to watch that she doesn't follow through with her threat to smuggle him home in her suitcase.

*****

May 2018

So, as I write the final words of this book, it is 26 May and Darakht's official birthday. We have chosen to celebrate each year on the date we brought him home. It was Dave's idea and a very fitting one, I think. It is another warm May day and Darakht still likes to lie in the dirt. I guess you can take a dog out of Afghanistan but some habits die hard.

A year on, Darakht will still happily walk out in front of an approaching vehicles yet the hoover, hairdryer and watering cans are still a deep source of anxiety. He runs away from waves and won't venture into any body of water above the tops of his legs, despite the fact that they're quite high off the ground, as you can imagine.

We've bought our tickets for the November 2018 Nowzad event which is at The Audley again. This year we will eat in the pub before we go down to the basement bar. I expect we'll also meet a few fellow adopters to chat to. Messages are also starting to fly around Facebook about Woofstock 2018 which is taking place in early August. We're already going so the opportunity to meet more adopters, catch up with the few we've met in person and swap stories feels like a great privilege.

Darakht's fundraising page is still live and I occasionally revisit it to remind myself of how far he has come in a relatively short space of time. It always rekindles the emotions I felt as the money poured in and how touched we were by generous donations from people we have never even met.

However, adopting a rescue dog from Afghanistan is not for everybody and they need a lot of love and attention to fully adjust to their new and unfamiliar surroundings. This has certainly been our experience and Darakht found it very hard to be a pet for the first few months. There have been no end of incidents including the nipping and mouthing of friends, family and random strangers alike.

He has pooed in various houses, destroyed some lovely bowls we bought in Vietnam and unraveled a hammock my friend Lucy brought back from Mexico for my 30th birthday. It seems that objects remain untouched for a long time are suddenly of interest to him. I do wonder if this is because he's picked up mine or Dave's scent as it always seems to be things we've touched recently.

The leather pouffe we bought on honeymoon in Marrakesh has also been ripped open, but he can probably smell the goat skin so I can't blame him too much on this one. He's eaten raw and cooked eggs meant for our breakfast, many freshly-prepared sandwiches, cheese our friend Maz bought us from Geneva, 900g blocks of cheese and uncooked pizza including its plastic wrapping to name a few. But, in the grand scheme of things they are just food and possessions and nobody died. And, regardless of his behavior at times it's a long game and we'll get there. Having him in our lives is endlessly rewarding and paid off in how affectionate and trusting he's become, in how protective and loyal he is.

Some people still look at us like we're mad when we tell them about how can to have Darakht, but we know what we have. He really is a beautiful dog and deserves all the love and attention we can give him. I feel so proud to be able to say we are Nowzad adopters and that we too can say we were able to help 'one dog at a time[3]'.

*****

---

[3] www.nowzad.com

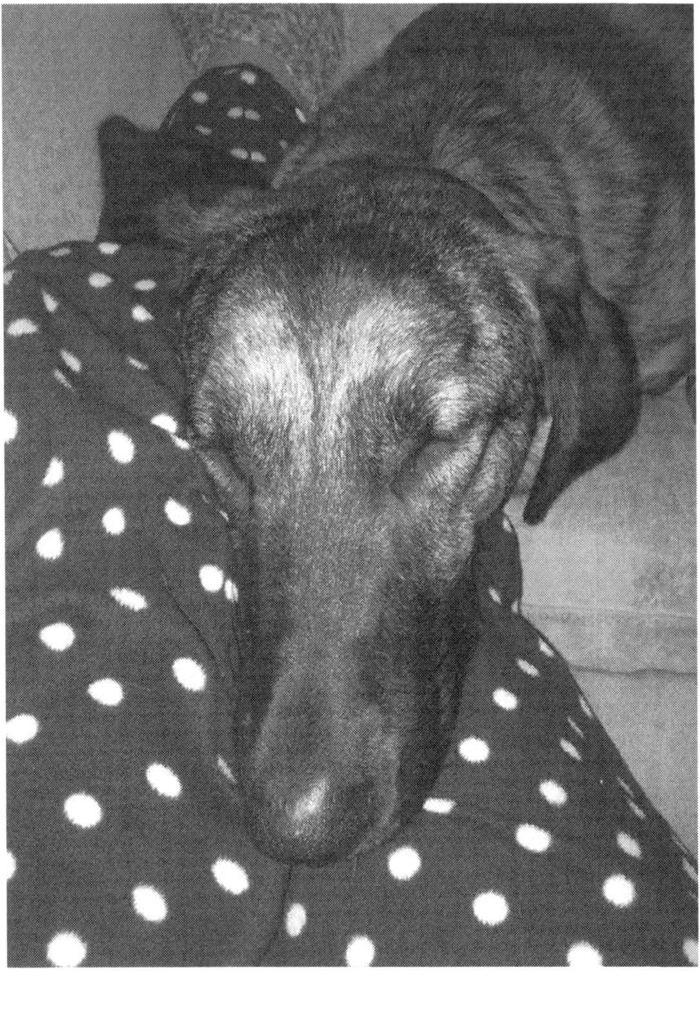

A Brief History of the Nowzad Charity

In November 2006, 42 Commando arrive in Helmand Province, Afghanistan to begin a six-month tour. The mission of Sergeant Paul 'Pen' Farthing and his fellow Royal Marines is clear: to provide security for the local people during a period of increasing insecurity and instability. However, it becomes apparent very quickly that the canine population is also desperately in need of their help.

Now Zad, the nearest town to their compound, is a hostile place. Teeming with stray dogs, but it isn't until Pen stumbles upon an organised dog fight that the scale of the problem becomes apparent. The animal that he risks his own life to rescue from this dog fight. Unbeknown to Pen, his Mum has contacted her local paper and, as a result, various donations flood in. Pen now has enough funds to arrange transport for five adult dogs and 11 puppies to the only Afghan rescue center. 300 miles away. The rest is history. If you're interested in learning about what happens next, read One Dog at a Time.

Nowzad: Nemesis of Noxious Dog Fighting

"To relieve the suffering of animals in Afghanistan; including companion animals, working equines, stray and abandoned dogs and cats and all other animals in need of care and attention, and to provide and maintain rescue, rehabilitation and education facilities for the care and treatment of such animals with no voice but ours".

- Nowzad's Mission Statement

Nowzad runs the only official animal shelter in the whole of Afghanistan. The charity is supported by a modern veterinary clinic staffed by a team of Afghan nationals who tirelessly care for animals in distress. They have created the first ever donkey sanctuary in the country, their vital work now includes animal welfare education and the prevention of the spread of rabies.

The fantastic support they have from animal lovers the world over who generously donate their time to promote and fund the work of the charity. This enables Nowzad to continue to support the brave men and women who 'show compassion to animals during their deployment' in addition to now rehoming the animals with families. Nowzad sprang from one man's efforts to make a difference for one dog at a time in Helmand Province, Afghanistan, dubbed the most dangerous place on Earth at the time[4].

Pen and Nowzad in Helmand Province, Afghanistan

---

[4] www.nowzad.com

Animal Welfare in Afghanistan

November to March is dog fighting season in Afghanistan when (it is said) their wounds heal more quickly due to the colder weather.

There are untold numbers of dogs whose ears and tails have been cruelly hacked off (without anaesthetic) in order to make them 'better fighters' in a country which heralds a centuries old 'tradition' of organised fighting.

These brutal contests are illegal. But due to their prestige and popularity, the amount of money and powerful people involved, Afghan authorities have done little to enforce any sort of ban. And, despite being haraam, dog fighting is widespread; even the Taliban have not succeeded in eradicating it.

Many dog owners attend fights on Fridays, a national holiday. Afghan herding dogs and Mastiffs are most commonly used in the competitive fights where winners can command upwards of $10,000 in prize money.

Whilst these hulking dogs risk great injury they do not usually fight until death. Often the battle will only finish when one dog pins down another, or one runs away or retreats with its tail between its legs.

The internet is awash with images of vicious looking dogs fighting at public matches of a traditional 'sport' banned as 'un-Islamic' by the Taliban, but which has now experienced a resurgence in popularity. Animal welfare is a foreign concept in Afghanistan.

Many Afghan people also consider contact with dogs to be haraam[5], although the only specific prohibition in the Qur'an is that dogs should not be kept inside the house. This helps fuel the popularity of the matches. Even so, dogs get a pretty raw deal, scavenging for food among refuse and surviving on their wits. Like a large proportion of the several thousand stray dogs that roam Kabul, living

---

[5] *anything prohibited in the Qu'ran or considered a sin if committed by a Muslim, e.g. adultery, murder or money from cheating or stealing. It can also apply to food or drink, such as pork or alcohol.*

in sewers and on the streets, Darakht could so easily have begun life on a rubbish tip in the city.

*****

Afghanistan in 2018: the current picture

The 13-year war in Afghanistan took the lives of more than 450 British servicemen, more than any other overseas military commitment in the past 50 years. Whilst life for many of the country's street dogs is much safer thanks to Nowzad, Pen, Hannah and the team carry on regardless, risking their lives to help the animals nobody else will.

In 2015, the Taliban retook Now Zad. In November 2017, Nowzad celebrated its 11th Anniversary in London. In 2018, the US deployed 10,000 troops. But, in the wake of resurging violence in Afghanistan and with new challenges including heroin-addicted dogs, it is even more vital that we draw attention to the charity in any way possible.

*****

Acknowledgments

I would like to thank my husband Dave for supporting me every step of the way and my Mum and Dad for the countless times they have looked after Darakht so far, especially the panicky last-minute requests.

Pen Farthing – thank you for writing your books in the first place and allowing us to adopt one of your amazing dogs. 10% of all sales of this book will be donated to the charity. And thank you for allowing me to use some of the images - all photographs have been reproduced with permission from the Nowzad charity.

Darakht – our very own Afghan Street Hound. We will love and care for you for as long as you'll let us.

Useful links & information

www.nowzad.com

www.justgiving.com/nowzaddogs

www.welllivedlifewithless.com

Printed in Great Britain
by Amazon